TERTIARY COLOURS:
A POST-TRAUMATIC VERSE
AARON KENT

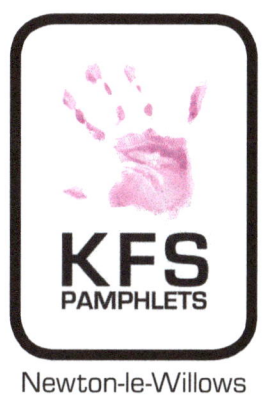

Newton-le-Willows

Published in the United Kingdom in 2018
by The Knives Forks And Spoons Press,
51 Pipit Avenue,
Newton-le-Willows,
Merseyside,
WA12 9RG.

ISBN 978-1-912211-27-2

Copyright © Aaron Kent, 2018.

The right of Aaron Kent to be identified as the author of this work has been asserted by them in accordance with the Copyrights, Designs and Patents Act of 1988. All rights reserved. No part of this publication may be reproduced, stored in a retrieval system, transmitted in any form or by any means, electronic, photocopying, recording or otherwise, without prior permission of the publisher.

Acknowledgements:

This book first and foremost goes out to my wife Emma Kennedy – who has made me who I am today, who was the first person I could speak to about my past, and who is still my favourite part of this world.

To Rue Frances Scout Kennedy – you cry a lot but I still love you.

To Jennifer Edgecombe, the world's greatest poetry editor.

Also to Frances Leake and Elizabeth Kennedy for making me feel welcome and a member of their family.

To Marc Willoughby, Laura Willoughby, Corella Hughes, Marcus Williamson, Sarah Perry, Philip Lyons, Lee Pountney, Steve Bowyer (both of you), Lina Helvik, Felicia 'Alabama' Weston, Ida Olsen, Ryan Lang, Kingsley Marshall, Rupert Loydell, Annabel Banks, Nan and Bampy.

To Rebekah Jones – founding member of 'The Now'.

To Jake Loewendahl for ensuring I could make it to London.

To CRASAC (Cornwall Rape and Sexual Assault Centre) who have revived me and deserve every plaudit available for the amazing (but underfunded) work they do.

To Tigs, Django, Millie.

To Haruki Murakami, Kanye West, Paul Auster, Claudia Rankine, Elliott Smith, Dean Young, Kim Addonizio, J. H. Prynne, Bruce Springsteen, Edwin Brock, Godzilla, Jacques Cousteau.

For my wife, Emma

*'If I am a bracelet on a thin, aging wrist,
you, princess, you are the charms.'*

And

*For those who lie awake at night
trying to kill their demons.*

TERTIARY COLOURS:
A POST-TRAUMATIC VERSE

I

When I wake I am bound to it, crying out for rapid eye movement, for beautiful sleep architecture. I am wed to my dreams and watching Operation Antler from the other side of the Danube – where our cats present mice as if the world just needs a little blood, and a bow. I sit absent at the breakfast table and spill my secrets to the toast, the jam, the darling black coffee. I reel off problems to present to the pandas in the broken men's club, chilled windows and broken radiators breathe winter into my hooves. My head prepares to split and welcome a new spring.

The horn comes
before the eye.

II

I pull slowly away from inability under the madness of infinity, and wear the charms under the weight of midday. With warmth comes effort, comes glory, comes a supreme release from an effective frame of reference (Kent, A., 1989. *Post-Traumatic: A Study of Engaging* with the Joy of Terror. Redruth: St Day Road). Tertiary colours exist for the covers of discontinued poetry books, and the moods of forgotten sailors. There are warnings in the shape of broken branches and migraines.

Tissue
replaces cartilage

III

The editor suggests brown bread works better / and a poached egg is marginally more romantic than a fried egg – some metaphor about the glory / of reproduction / I'm ignorant / clawing / the sharpened edges of my sister's retreat / into the neighbouring crooked hill / I find solace / in pen marks / little notes / and a dictionary / with no pages / I have superglue for fingers / and wear my clothes with all the grace of a dying man / phone lines are designed to catch people / who lean out of train windows.

The bone is infected
by osteoclasts.

I am Perseus in somnambulance [again] / caught in daydreams / of auxiliary machinery spaces where a career touch / burns hydraulic and bleeds ballast / we broke cardinal rules / fell victim to cardinals / the ceiling is glass in tertiary / colours / stained with my mentor's nuclear fluid / radiation / is a plague of numbers / 51°22'47.1"N 30°06'50.6"E / a protective measure / a hand straying / through the exclusion zone / a muffled scream / I lean out of the window / and feel summer brush the top of the glass.

IV

I crawl disfigured into kintsugi, hear the pikatrapp chimes call me for Geppetto. There is little fight left, and trace amounts of salt. I am unbound, treading water in military overalls disguising

        a three-piece suit. The charms wear tired eyes, a sign they have ingested too much today: all two hundred meters of water drawn from a flood in Tolgus to a death in an Atlantic prison.

        I will not sleep in blue skies when there are genes to wear as a raincoat. My skull reforms, I am no longer wrapped in gold. The psychic

        who warned me of angels the size of houses has clearly never sat in a library and read the old dreams of unicorn skulls.

Something else for the dog
to chew on.

V

I sit as a representation of Piaget's refusal to repeat generations, watching solar powered windmills direct traffic across the sjóndeildarhnífuringur. Methods to reject introspection include:
pretending to know how to meditate,
glorifying failures,
burning through the night.
I close my eyes and let the reservoir fill with sharks and hate, remnants of a tin mine past – that dance of crimson on my inner canthal has betrayed me, led me back down the grey tiled garden. I'm striking bark at midnight, striking the rats from the torpedoes, sutoraiku two inches from nuclear destruction. There are two cinemas showing *The Sopranos*, neither lets me in, I'm left to drink wine from the tap.

VI

Broken hands and broken mouths. Regret and resentment and hand-washed clothes.

From the French
meaning before
the eye. Antoillier.

VII

With fear and glory in equal measure.

VIII

There's a vague sense of my mother / carrying me above snakes / my head bowed to the sound of an operator / begging for another chance to revive the child / a hint of my brother / breaking my heart / a daughter who grew up too fast – became a robot.

    Became a feature of the room, some jewelled ornament.

I'm never in the same room when I wake / sometimes there are sixty seven seats / other times I'm ironing / in the kitchen rubbing soap on the inside of my seams / they won't catch me biting through pistachio shells / spitting sunflowers / into our cemeteries – there's a tree nobody can touch / it's too famous.

    A tree for an ambient airport.

My back aches from carrying the charms / through needles and nettles / there was a pickaxe / in the cabin / a spray of blood and ninety degrees / of indecision / we hid in the background / and found heaven at the bottom of a manhole / I choked her for protection / forced my arm into the bars / at the top of the bed / there were malicious men, damaged crooks, broken thieves / who wanted glory / I poured myself into her / forced their knives / into my back / kept the embryo golden.

    I am not meant to carry gold / just to throw it on the beauty.

I lost sight of the doorway and clung to the sheets / a state of construction / as my mind wept daylight across my retina / the editor remembers / where the walls were, but moves them three inches / inwards – claustrophobia is an interesting trait / the editor / wants me to choose a Windsor knot / relate it to my daddy issues / maybe a story about a job interview.

    "Your dad never taught you to shave / tie a tie / ride a bike"

…yes / unprepared / and covered / in the stench of his ink.

IX

I saw myself in Rough Park,
        floating
                unaided
                      using the same lines over and over.
I never meant to be repetitive,
        to lock myself away
                with the broken records
                      scratched firmly against *pikatrapp*.

X

The cat knows what I'm trying to say, the rhyme scheme I've given up on, and the words I can't mouth [even in my healthiest friendship circle]. I no longer hear foxes at night and I worry it's because they thought I was a voyeur. I watched them tear apart the bins in the hope of finding my name and address, stealing my identity, then having to deal with all my repressed torment. Theories of glasses being half full or empty ignore the fact that somebody has to pour the liquid in, and I forget to drink some days. Most days. Forget to breathe some times. Most times. Forget to tell new people that I was touched by some dude in some way. A wholly inappropriate way. I'd like to see the foxes deal with that.

Nutritional dependency
has caused me to fall apart
again.

XI

Demons sit in the dentist's waiting room, picking the sand from their teeth and I watch my addiction to black coffee form a perfect black sphere in the centre of my iris. I wake sober in the city centre and plan an ancient God's murder by forgiving every Krossdeath.

I am discarded
as calcium and phosphorus.

I begin a new obsession with tape recorders, so I can play my thoughts back every Thursday to the kintsugi club. 'Note to self: His hand was clammy. Note to self: You can still smell the grease on his neck at night. Note to self: He followed you back on that flight from Glasgow to Cornwall.'

I am hunted: Beam, palm, brow, bez
or bay, trez or tray, royal, and surroyal.

I serve an arabica – robusta blend to the family with the toothpaste smiles, and wonder what would happen if they introduced me to their hero. A man with a kind nature, a good heart, and the stench of my shame still ironed into his epaulets.

XII

Even
        in
        winter
                the
        sky
still glows
                for
        a man
                with
                        too many
                suns
to
        notice
                the disappearance
of
a
single
                jigsaw
                                                            star.

XIII

I am most spectacular in convalescence / of the night sky / when I break the shell / in search of silence as a plot device / I count the seconds / where the morning has not yet leeched joy / from the rheum in my retina / at nine weeks the eyes fuse shut / and with nine hours I sew mine together / use thread from a torn duvet and stitch my world's finale / the brightest lights / are immune to my caffeine withdrawal / I keep killing / my djöfaðirullin in REM sleep.

All I ever wanted was candles / on a birthday cake.

Give me velvet / antlers.

XIV

When I climb stairs I *pikatrapp pikatrapp.* When I climb stairs I remain silent.

XV

When I leave the broken club [the kintsugi starts to form] and the stories begin to dissipate, I am reminded of how little testosterone I have left after he tore it from my system. I walk through the watchmaker's alley, and rekindle my sorry excuses. I could never kill my God, could never leave the stairs, could never break his hydraulic hand before he became hydraulic. AMS II/III is still deep in my flesh, still whispering shrapnel in my ear and cleaning wounds in his bunk. I keep my hands soft, don't let dirt cling to them [won't piss with dirty fingers because it may feel like his grip again, the coarseness of his flesh, the dexterity of his digits]. Is this what a novel is supposed to look like? I consider changing the scope of the story, make it less biographical, a pseudo-biopic with a happy ending. Instead of tearing out my soul, we could've sat down with a cup of coffee – brewed a mug of arabica and opened up. He'd tell me he wanted to violate me, smash my back, and squeeze my throat. We could discuss what this really means for him, the ways in which he could better himself *[next time make a list of the ways you want to scar me for life, but read it aloud once to yourself and throw it away after]*. He could have two sugars, I could have none, he could make the joke that I'm sweet enough, and I'd live safe in the knowledge that it was just a joke, not an invitation to unzip my flies and rain nuclear waste down upon me. But writing is sometimes honest, sometimes true, sometimes a reason for an exorcism. So I keep in the finer points, ignore the trivial need for fictionalisation, and burn the fragments that encourage mediocrity.

*I was reclaimed
to build him a gun,
to build him a dagger.*

XVI

When I watch the charms find glory in the dead of night, I capture every mark on her face. I make imprints of our potential and determine that with enough luck maybe I won't burden our child with much of my DNA at all.

XVII

My favourite part was when I kicked the walls until I bled because I swore I saw a door there.
I have seen men with knives carve my name into deaths they had sewn in the wallpaper.

I watched my brother choke from the weight of the roof, sans hurricane, sans life.
There are always spiders, always tarantulas, always the size of small cars.

Sometimes snakes remind me I pissed the bed until I was twelve.
When the room caves in I leap to the defence of the dead.

My hobbies involve watching as strangers' eyes bleed.
I've become an expert at breaking my knuckles

but you've become spectacular at holding me
until I stop crying, and lulling me back

to sleep.

XVIII

I am informed there aren't enough colours, not enough title-nodding references, or little nudges between the reader and the ideas presented. The editor wants something a little more oblique, a little less opaque. Let the reader watch you / dissolve.

He wore his pride aloft as horns.

XIX

I had never been primary / enough to paint the sky / in broad strokes / just a tertiary colour burnt from the brush / of a broken hand / the mood of forgotten sailors / mermaids as medusa (Hayter, C., 1826. *A New Practical Treatise on the Three Primitive Colours Assumed as a Perfect System of Rudimentary Information.* London).

XX

With fear and glory embalmed in a house in Redruth.

XXI

You are not the sum of your parts, or the collection of news stories some western media thinks will sell front pages to bored conspiracy theorists. You were, and still are, a kid torn from Bangladesh and promised a brighter start in southwest England. You were a couple of years older, but put in our class, and you were quick to gain friends. You gave us free meals at your restaurant, and we gave you immunity from the idiocy of children taught by parasites to hate. You wore the same backpack every day, and you never quite learnt to look both ways before crossing the road. You were welcomed and loved. You were an important part of my childhood. You were mocked by my mother – who looked both ways and crossed the road when she saw you with that backpack, or joked that you should leave it outside the house for fear that it contained a bomb. My mum, the white, suburban, bored conspiracy theorist who swore she believed in God.

There is no genetic correlation.

XXII

I still write lyrics for a friend, and every time I struggle to write pop in a way that warrants mainstream interest. I want to write of torture, and car batteries, and shots of whiskey, and the glory of fatherly stubble, and broken arms, and broken wings, and torn feathers, and blisters, and triangular junctions, and pika, and trapp, and the fate of a defeatist childhood, and living room truces, and renegade brothers, and frozen ground, and marked men, and forced dancing, and drug-addled weightlifting, and speed in cakes, and Hell's Angels, and shanking people in Acton, and a Hungarian man trying to make a difference, and noses pushed to ceilings, and backs slapping floors, and hands pressed tight to radiators, and Princess Diana taking over all the TV channels, and Muhammad's backpack, and tin Skodas, and Hey Arnold as a genuine depiction of family, and the blues, and the Blues, and the holly bush, and the drunk neighbours, and the stoned neighbours, and the stabbed neighbours, and scooter rallies, and grill pans, and the memory of sex toys, and ironing at five am, and sleeping at three am, and waking at four am, and falling down stairs still asleep, and breaking toes, and breaking a finger, and breaking my heart, and the dogs who were never walked, and auxiliary machine space number two on the third level, and some chief, and the mind's ability to block things out, and Grandad on breathing equipment, and locked in a caravan by the beach, and bedroom floors at Christmas, and the babysitter, and the old friend, and my sister's mum, and my sister, and those eighteen lost years, and the inability to cry, and the pillow of my face, and bipolar with no support, and

I think it's probably time I stop
writing about this shit but I can't
but I can't
but I can't
but I can't
and I still blame you in every
way, in every moment I have
free I blame you for the mess I
have made of things.

XXIII

...and it was there you presented / didn't wait for a response / your strength on display / your fertility ready to squeeze / tight / your overgrown antlers / my underwhelming tertiary colours / we fought / I lost / you took your prize amongst the blood / and / diesel / I can't remember if I swelled from the bruises / or stayed limp from fear / but for a moment I turned red / I was primary / I became singular / and all it needed was a lack of consent / and a cut that wouldn't stop bleeding.

My velvet – lost

My bones – dead

My experience – the footnote of a short trip across the Atlantic.

XXIV

When I wake / I am still bound to it, begging for sleep architecture from a fashion magazine. I am the moods of forgotten sailors, picking the superglue from broken fingers, broken toes. Mount Amara bound, your radiation was a curse, and the charms brought summer to translucent windows – more can be ingested today, but never pikatrapp. I wrapped the bed in gold but still found djöfaðirullin on the sjóndeildarhnífuringur where angels the size of car tires carried me over snakes. [still hating the fifth and sixth, still mad at cheap tricks]. [am happier with the fifth, now love the sixth]. With glory and a robot daughter leaving ambient airports for a shot at freedom. Floating unaided, always locked away. I forget to fill my lungs while the foxes have left from the boredom of begging me to breathe again. Krossdeath has never been the excuse I needed it to be, it never boarded a flight to my witness protection, it never wore my shame like a medal I couldn't receive. Even in winter I repeat myself. I'm rebuilding for the future, splicing my genes with the charms and a bright vessel to fill with hope. To put candles in their birthday cake. I watched my brother choke my presence from his life and still didn't call enough attention to the colour palette of famous artists. The bruises still leak into my skin, and you still caress me in my most anxious hours. When I climb stairs I am reminded of cameras, and oak and a promise not to tell anyone because they'd be angry, and you'd be in a lot of trouble.

Without antlers
I'll grow tusks.

Aaron Kent

Djöfaðirullin Parade

There is a fire
in the corner
of
the care
home,
and I will never
douse it
or let you light
cigarettes
on the edge of the ash
or flames.

It exists
purely
as a tutorial,
a light on the sjóndeildarhuringur
to show you
how to join
the djöfaðirullin parade
when your wnigs
are nothing but
the cancerous
stumps
of a forgotten goat herder.

Love me in ways
that the Beach Boys

can never
sing
about
because
the hallucinogenics
aren't strong enough
to warp
camera flashes
into signs of better
men.
There is no reason
to find sanity
in the corner
of
a broken bathtub.

You are the weakness
I cradle at night
and the rapidfire
in my lungs,
you are every
locked door
on a hospital ward,
and you are more
than just
a mistake
Guð pressed
into the book
that holds
my hourglass.

www.ingramcontent.com/pod-product-compliance
Lightning Source LLC
Chambersburg PA
CBHW041632040426
42446CB00023B/3491